HAL•LEONARD®
CELLO
PLAY-ALONG

AUDIO
ACCESS
INCLUDED

LOVE SONGS

VOL 7

PLAYBACK+
Speed • Pitch • Balance • Loop

To access audio visit:
www.halleonard.com/mylibrary

Enter Code
1116-2205-6022-3523

ISBN 978-1-4950-8572-7

Trischa Loebl, cello
Audio arrangements by Peter Deneff
Recorded and Produced at Beat House Music, Milwaukee, Wisconsin

HAL•LEONARD®
7777 W. BLUEMOUND RD. P.O. BOX 13819 MILWAUKEE, WI 53213

Visit Hal Leonard Online at
www.halleonard.com

Can't Help Falling in Love

from the Paramount Picture BLUE HAWAII

Words and Music by George David Weiss, Hugo Peretti and Luigi Creatore

Fields of Gold

Music and Lyrics by Sting

Hey There Delilah

Words and Music by Tom Higgenson

Longer

Words and Music by Dan Fogelberg

My Heart Will Go On
(Love Theme from 'Titanic')

from the Paramount and Twentieth Century Fox Motion Picture TITANIC

Music by James Horner
Lyric by Will Jennings

Wonderful Tonight

Words and Music by Eric Clapton

Your Song

Words and Music by Elton John and Bernie Taupin

You Are So Beautiful

Words and Music by Billy Preston and Bruce Fisher